soup

COMFORT FOOD

soup

COMFORT FOOD

CHARLES PIERCE

Andrews McMeel
Publishing

Kansas City

Comfort Food: Soup copyright © 1997 by Smallwood & Stewart, Inc. All rights reserved. Printed in Singapore. No part of this book may be used or reproduced in any manner whatsoever without written permission except in the case of reprints in context of reviews. For information, write Andrews McMeel Publishing, an Andrews McMeel Universal company, 4520 Main Street, Kansas City, Missouri 64111. www.andrewsmcmeel.com

ISBN: 0-8362-5114-8

Library of Congress Catalog Card Number: 97-73616

First Edition

1 2 3 4 5 6 7 8 9 10

Produced by Smallwood & Stewart, Inc., New York City

Editor: Deborah Mintcheff

Copy Editor: Judith Sutton

Designer: Susi Oberhelman

Design Assistant: Ayako Hosono

Photographer: Steven Mark Needham

Food Stylist: William Smith

Jacket photograph: Mediterranean Fish Soup

Back jacket photograph: Minestrone

Page 2 photograph: Summer Tomato, Corn & Okra Soup

table of contents

Soup is without a doubt the ultimate comfort food. Whether it's a simple, clear broth or an exotic variation brimming with enticing ingredients, the taste, texture, and deeply satisfying aroma of a favorite soup seems to linger in our memory long after the meal. A lusty bowl of *Lentil Soup with Sausages* or delicately spiced *Carrot and Ginger Soup* served in a favorite cup will nourish and warm, and a bowl of *Gazpacho* will refresh on the hottest of summer days.

Everybody loves soup and nearly all of us have comforting childhood memories associated with it. My own childhood was spent in Georgia where we

were often served a soup laden with garden-fresh butter beans, plump tomatoes, okra, and lots of just-picked corn. Served with warm cornbread for supper, it was a family favorite which assured my mother that we were eating a healthful dose of vegetables.

My taste in soup didn't really grow until I traveled in Europe and was fortunate enough to spend some time at an estate in Burgundy. The vegetable garden was abundant and it was inevitable that I would be introduced to the glory of potato and leek soup. No matter how many times I was served this soup, I eagerly awaited the next. It was simply perfect food. I also traveled to Portugal where I came to adore *Caldo Verde*. Like minestrone in Italy, this nationally beloved soup comes in a thousand variations and is found on every restaurant menu. The base ingredient is always dark, leafy greens which reminded me of the thick, bitter mustard and turnip greens so familiar to me and anyone else who grew up below the Mason-Dixon line.

From simple soups with friends to incredible creations in three-star restaurants, my love affair with soup hasn't faded because soup can take on innumerable guises. Be it cold and silky smooth, light and low-fat, or indulgently rich and creamy, it is a welcome addition to a meal, or anytime in between. *Pumpkin-Leek Soup* and *Creamy Cauliflower Soup*, for example, are ideal preludes to a festive holiday dinner; *Hungarian Goulash Soup* and *Cod and Leek Chowder* adapt easily to the role of hearty one-dish supper, and *Cheddar Cheese Soup* and *Roasted Red Pepper and Cumin Soup* just as gracefully round out a light lunch with friends. Soup can be prepared with simple ingredients that happen to be on hand, or be as exotic as your imagination and local gourmet market allow. And when fresh local ingredients are in high season, soup is the perfect way to celebrate the best of nature's bounty.

The collection of favorite recipes I offer here includes a wonderful variety of soups. I hope that you get as much enjoyment from preparing and partaking of them as I have had in sharing them with you.

carrot & ginger soup

Carrot soup is ideal as part of a light lunch or first course for a holiday dinner. For an interesting variation, substitute cubed, peeled sweet potatoes in place of the carrots to create an equally luscious soup.

In a large pot, combine the carrots, onion, and oil. Cook over medium-high heat, stirring, for about 3 minutes, or until the onion begins to soften. Stir in the flour and cook for 2 minutes. Pour in the broth, season with salt and pepper, and bring to a boil over high heat. Reduce the heat to medium and cook, stirring occasionally, for about 20 minutes, or until the carrots are tender. Stir in the ginger.

In a food processor or blender, puree the soup in batches. Return the soup to the pot and season to taste with salt and pepper if necessary. Gently reheat, ladle into bowls, and garnish with the parsley. **SERVES 6**

2 pounds carrots, finely chopped

1 medium-size onion, chopped

2 tablespoons olive oil

2 tablespoons all-purpose flour

4 cups chicken broth or stock (p. 70)

Salt & freshly ground pepper

One 2-inch piece fresh ginger, peeled & minced

1 tablespoon chopped fresh flat-leaf parsley

pea soup with lemon sour cream

½ cup sour cream

1 teaspoon grated lemon zest

Salt & freshly ground pepper

2 tablespoons unsalted butter

1 large onion, finely chopped

1 (10-ounce) package frozen peas, thawed

1 cup loosely packed fresh flat-leaf parsley leaves

2 cups chicken broth or stock (p. 70)

1 cup heavy cream

The secret to keeping the bright green color of this refreshing summer soup is to cook it uncovered.

In a small bowl, combine the sour cream and lemon zest, stirring well. Season with salt and pepper, cover with plastic wrap, and refrigerate.

In a large pot, melt the butter over medium-high heat. Add the onion and cook, stirring often, for 3 to 5 minutes, until softened. Add the peas and parsley and cook for 3 minutes. Pour in the broth, increase the heat to high, and bring to a boil. Season with salt and pepper, then boil rapidly for 5 minutes.

In a food processor or blender, puree the soup in batches. Return the soup to the pot and bring to a boil. Reduce the heat to medium and stir in the cream. Season to taste with salt and pepper if necessary and gently simmer for 5 minutes, or until heated through. Ladle the soup into small bowls and garnish with dollops of the lemon sour cream. **SERVES 6**

shrimp & artichoke soup

The addition of a few spinach leaves or a small handful of fresh parsley just before pureeing will further enhance the flavor and color of this springtime soup.

In a large nonreactive pot, melt the butter with the oil over medium-high heat. Add the shrimp and cook, stirring constantly, for 2 to 3 minutes, until pink. Transfer the shrimp to a small bowl and cover.

Add the onion to the pot and cook, stirring often, for 3 minutes, or until softened. Add the artichoke hearts and cook for 2 minutes. Pour in the clam juice, wine, and water. Increase the heat to high and bring to a boil. Season with salt and pepper and cook for 5 minutes, or until the artichokes are tender.

In a food processor or blender, puree the soup in batches. Return the soup to the pot and cook over medium-high heat until heated through. Stir in the shrimp and season to taste with salt and pepper if necessary. Ladle into bowls and garnish with the lemon slices. **SERVES 4 TO 6**

2 tablespoons unsalted butter

2 tablespoons vegetable oil

1 pound medium-size shrimp, peeled, deveined & cut into ¼-inch pieces

1 large onion, chopped

2 (9-ounce) packages frozen artichoke hearts, thawed

2 (8-ounce) bottles clam juice or 2 cups fish stock (p. 73)

1 cup dry white wine

1 cup cold water

Salt & freshly ground pepper

Paper-thin lemon slices, for garnish

chilled cucumber mint soup

2 medium-size cucumbers (about ¾ pound), peeled, halved & seeded

2 cups well chilled plain yogurt *(see Note)*

¼ cup chopped fresh mint, plus whole mint leaves, for garnish

Salt & freshly ground pepper

NOTE

Full fat, low-fat, or nonfat yogurt all work well in this refreshing soup.

Serve this cooling soup as part of a meal of grilled butterflied leg of lamb and couscous salad. For the best results, be sure to squeeze out as much moisture as possible from the cucumbers before combining them with the yogurt.

Coarsely grate the cucumbers. Using your hands, gently squeeze out the excess liquid. In a medium-size bowl, combine the cucumbers and yogurt. Stir in the mint and season with salt and pepper. Ladle into chilled bowls and garnish with mint leaves. **SERVES 4**

variation

Chopped fresh dill can be added to the soup along with the mint, or can be substituted for the mint for equally delicious results.

tomato & white bean soup

¼ **pound bacon**

2 carrots, chopped

1 onion, chopped

1 celery stalk, chopped

1 garlic clove, minced

1 (28-ounce) can whole tomatoes, drained & coarsely chopped

1 (15½-ounce) can Great Northern or cannellini beans, drained & rinsed

2 cups chicken broth or stock (p. 70)

2 cups cold water

1 tablespoon chopped fresh thyme or 1 teaspoon dried thyme

Salt & freshly ground pepper

In late summer, when fresh tomatoes are at their peak, substitute about four ripe medium-size tomatoes for the canned.

Cook the bacon in a large nonreactive pot over medium heat until crisp and browned. Drain on a paper towel–lined plate. When cool enough to handle, finely chop and set aside.

Pour off and discard all but 2 tablespoons of the bacon fat. Add the carrots, onion, and celery and cook over medium-high heat, stirring, for 5 minutes, or until the onion is softened. Add the garlic and cook for 1 minute. Stir in the tomatoes, beans, broth, water, and thyme. Increase the heat to high and bring to a boil. Reduce the heat and simmer for 10 to 15 minutes, until the carrots are tender. Season with salt and pepper.

In a food processor or blender, puree the soup in batches. Return the soup to the pot and season to taste with salt and pepper if necessary. Reheat, then ladle into bowls, and sprinkle with the bacon. **SERVES 4**

cheddar cheese soup

This is a satisfying cold-weather soup with a velvety smooth texture and rich, mellow flavor. It makes an easy lunch served with a romaine lettuce and tomato salad, and warm, crusty country-style bread.

In a large pot, melt the butter over medium-high heat. Stir in the flour and cook, stirring often, for about 3 minutes, or until bubbling and smooth. Pour in the broth, increase the heat to high, and bring to a boil. Cook, stirring often, for 3 to 5 minutes, until thickened and smooth. Reduce the heat to medium and add the cheese, stirring constantly, until melted. Do not let the soup boil, or it will curdle. Pour in the milk, whisking until smooth. Add the ground red pepper and season with salt and pepper. Reheat gently, ladle into bowls, and sprinkle with the tomato. **SERVES 4**

2 tablespoons unsalted butter

3 tablespoons all-purpose flour

2 cups beef broth or stock (p. 79)

2 cups grated sharp cheddar cheese (8 ounces)

1 cup milk

$\frac{1}{8}$ teaspoon ground red pepper, or to taste

Salt & freshly ground pepper

1 small tomato, cut into $\frac{1}{4}$-inch dice, for garnish

cod & leek chowder

2 tablespoons unsalted butter

2 medium-size leeks (white part only), thinly sliced & washed well

¾ pound Yukon Gold potatoes, peeled & cut into ½-inch cubes

3 cups cold water

1 cup dry white wine

1½ pounds cod fillet, skin removed & cut into large chunks

Salt & freshly ground pepper

Although this classic chowder is traditionally prepared with cod, other firm-fleshed fish such as bass, sea trout, whiting, or halibut will do very nicely.

In a large nonreactive pot, melt the butter over medium-high heat. Add the leeks and potatoes and cook, stirring often, for about 5 minutes, or until the leeks are slightly softened. Add the water and wine, increase the heat to high, and bring to a boil. Reduce the heat to medium and cook for 10 to 15 minutes, until the potatoes are almost tender. Add the fish and cook for 5 to 7 minutes longer, until the fish is opaque throughout. Season to taste with salt and pepper, ladle into large shallow bowls, and serve. **SERVES 4 TO 6**

roasted red pepper & cumin soup

2 tablespoons olive oil

**2 (7-ounce) jars roasted
red peppers, drained
& chopped**

**1 small all-purpose potato
(4 to 6 ounces), peeled
& cubed**

**4 cups chicken stock
or broth (p. 70)**

1 teaspoon ground cumin

**Salt & freshly ground
pepper**

*This is a great soup for those of us trying
to keep our calorie count down. It contains
very little fat, but plenty of flavor.*

In a large heavy pot, heat the oil over medium-high heat. Add
the peppers and cook, stirring often, for 3 to 5 minutes, until
softened. Add the potato and cook for 5 minutes, or until slightly softened. Pour in the stock, increase the heat to high, and
bring to a boil. Reduce the heat to medium and simmer for 10
minutes, or until the peppers and potato are very tender. Stir
in the cumin and cook for 5 minutes longer.

In a food processor or blender, puree the soup in batches.
Return the soup to the pot and reheat. Season to taste with salt
and pepper and serve. **SERVES 4**

pumpkin-leek soup

Pumpkin and leeks, two of fall's best and often underused vegetables, are combined to create a simple and elegant soup—a sumptuous addition to any Thanksgiving menu.

In a large pot, melt the butter over medium-high heat. Add the onion and leeks and cook, stirring often, for 10 minutes, or until the leeks are softened. Stir in the pumpkin and cook for 2 to 3 minutes, until coated with the butter. Pour in enough stock to cover by 1 inch. Increase the heat to high and bring to a boil. Reduce the heat to medium and simmer for 15 to 20 minutes, until the pumpkin is very tender.

In a food processor or blender, puree the soup in batches. Return the soup to the pot, reheat, and season with salt and pepper. Ladle into bowls and sprinkle with the toasted pumpkin seeds. **SERVES 4 TO 6**

- **2 tablespoons unsalted butter**
- **1 small onion, finely chopped**
- **2 medium-size leeks (white part only), thinly sliced & washed well**
- **4 cups diced (½-inch) pumpkin**
- **4 to 6 cups chicken stock (p. 70)**
- **Salt & freshly ground pepper**
- **½ cup chopped toasted pumpkin seeds, for garnish**

creamy tomato soup with swirled basil

3 pounds tomatoes, peeled, seeded & coarsely chopped

BASIL ESSENCE

2 tablespoons olive oil

1 tablespoon red wine vinegar

1 tablespoon warm water

2 cups loosely packed fresh basil leaves

⅛ teaspoon salt

2 tablespoons olive oil

1 medium-size onion, chopped

1 celery stalk, thinly sliced

2 tablespoons all-purpose flour

1 cup chicken stock (p. 70) or vegetable stock (p. 77), plus additional if needed

A small amount of cream balances the acidity of the tomatoes and gives this ideal warm-weather soup a richer and more delicate flavor.

Put the tomatoes into a strainer set over a large bowl. Set aside for 30 to 40 minutes, until the tomato juices drain off.

Meanwhile, prepare the basil essence: In a measuring cup, combine the oil, vinegar, and warm water. Put the basil into a food processor. With the machine running, add the vinegar mixture and process until smooth, scraping down the sides of the bowl as needed. Add the salt and process until blended. Transfer the basil puree to a fine strainer set over a small bowl and press with the back of a spoon to extract as much of the liquid as possible; you should have about 2 tablespoons. If there is less, set the strainer with the basil over the bowl, add a little hot water, and strain the liquid into the bowl. Cover with plastic wrap and refrigerate.

In a large nonreactive pot, heat the oil over medium-high heat. Add the onion and celery and cook, stirring often, for 3

**Salt & freshly ground
pepper**

1 tablespoon tomato paste

1 teaspoon warm water

½ cup heavy cream

**Very small basil leaves,
for garnish**

minutes, or until the onion is softened. Sprinkle with the flour and cook, stirring, for 2 to 3 minutes, until the mixture is lightly browned. Add the tomatoes and stock, increase the heat to high, and bring to a boil, scraping to loosen any browned bits in the bottom of the pot. Season the soup with salt and pepper and cook, stirring often, for about 5 minutes, or until thickened.

In a small bowl, whisk the tomato paste into the warm water. Stir into the soup.

In a food processor or blender, puree the soup in batches. Pour the soup through a strainer set over a large bowl; discard the solids. You should have about 2½ cups. If necessary, add additional stock or water to equal this amount.

In a large saucepan, combine the soup and cream. Cook over medium-low heat, stirring gently, for about 5 minutes, or until heated through. Do not let the soup boil. Season to taste with salt and pepper if necessary. Ladle into bowls and garnish with a swirl of the basil essence and some basil leaves.

SERVES 4 TO 6

leek & potato soup

To turn this comforting, winter soup into a classic, summer vichyssoise, puree the soup, stir in some heavy cream, and refrigerate. Serve well-chilled in small bowls, sprinkled with snipped fresh chives.

In a large heavy saucepan, melt the butter over medium-high heat. Add the onion and cook, stirring, for 3 minutes, or until softened. Stir in the leeks and potatoes and reduce the heat to medium-low. Cover and cook, stirring often, for 10 minutes.

Pour in the stock, increase the heat to medium-high, and bring to a boil. Season the soup with salt and pepper. Reduce the heat and simmer for 20 to 30 minutes, until the leeks and the potatoes are very tender. Ladle into small bowls and serve.

SERVES 4 TO 6

- **2 tablespoons unsalted butter**
- **1 medium-size onion, chopped**
- **3 medium-size leeks, thinly sliced & washed well**
- **1 pound all-purpose potatoes, preferably Yukon Gold, peeled & thinly sliced**
- **4 cups chicken stock (p. 70) or broth**
- **Salt & freshly ground pepper**

spinach & chickpea soup

PITA CRISPS

Two 5-inch pita breads

2 tablespoons olive oil

¼ cup freshly grated Parmesan cheese

2 tablespoons olive oil

1 large onion, chopped

1 pound spinach, trimmed, washed well & coarsely chopped

2 medium-size tomatoes (about ½ pound), seeded & chopped

2 cups cooked chickpeas, drained & rinsed if canned

4 cups vegetable stock (p. 77) or broth

Salt & freshly ground pepper

2 tablespoons fresh lemon juice

Saute a thinly sliced small red bell pepper and add it to this Middle Eastern–style soup just before serving.

Prepare the pita crisps: Preheat the oven to 350°F. Brush the pita breads with the oil. Cut the breads in half, then cut each half into ½-inch-wide strips. Unfold each strip and cut in half.

In a large bowl, toss the pita strips with the cheese. Spread the strips in a single layer on a large baking sheet. Bake, turning once, for 5 to 7 minutes, until browned and crisp. Place the baking sheet on a wire rack to cool.

In a large heavy nonreactive pot, heat the oil over medium-high heat. Add the onion and cook, stirring, for 3 minutes, or until softened. Add the spinach and cook, stirring often, for 5 minutes, or until wilted. Stir in the tomatoes, chickpeas, and stock, and season with salt and pepper. Cook until just heated through. Do not overcook, or the spinach will lose its bright green color. Stir in the lemon juice and serve the soup in large shallow bowls, topped with the pita crisps. **SERVES 6**

double squash soup with roasted garlic puree

Make this soup in the summer when zucchini and yellow squash are most plentiful. Here, the two squash soups are cooked separately, ladled side by side into bowls, and topped with a spoonful of smoky roasted garlic puree. This is comfort food at its best.

Prepare the roasted garlic puree: Preheat the oven to 350°F.

Place the head of garlic on a square of foil and drizzle with 1 tablespoon of the oil. Fold the foil edges together to seal. Bake for 1 hour, or until very soft. Let the garlic cool in the foil. Gently squeeze the garlic pulp into a small bowl and blend in the lemon juice and the remaining 1 tablespoon oil. Season with salt and pepper and set aside.

Meanwhile, put the zucchini and yellow squash in separate large bowls, squeeze the lemon halves over, then sprinkle each with 1 teaspoon salt. Set aside, tossing often, for about 1 hour.

Roast the bell pepper over a gas flame, turning it, for 15 minutes, or until blackened. Transfer to a plastic bag, seal, and

ROASTED GARLIC PUREE

1 large head garlic

2 tablespoons olive oil

1 teaspoon fresh lemon juice

Salt & freshly ground pepper

1½ pounds each zucchini & yellow squash, cut into ½-inch dice

1 lemon, halved

Salt

1 large yellow bell pepper

3 tablespoons olive oil

2 medium-size onions, chopped

2 celery stalks, chopped

About 4 cups chicken stock (p. 70) or broth

Freshly ground pepper

let steam for 10 minutes. When cool enough to handle, peel, core, and seed the pepper, then cut into ½-inch dice.

Over medium heat, put 1½ tablespoons of the oil into each of two large pots. Add half the onion and celery to each pot. Cook, stirring, for 5 minutes, or until the onion is softened. Meanwhile, rinse the zucchini under cold running water, drain, and pat dry with paper towels. Repeat with the yellow squash.

Add the zucchini to one pot, and add the yellow squash and bell pepper to the other. Pour enough stock into each pot to barely cover and season with salt and pepper. Simmer for 10 minutes, or until the vegetables are tender.

Transfer the zucchini with its cooking liquid to a food processor or blender and process until smooth. Return the puree to the pot. Repeat with the yellow squash. Reheat both soups and season to taste with salt and pepper if necessary.

To serve, ladle some of the zucchini soup into one side of each bowl, then ladle some yellow squash soup into the other side. Top each serving with a teaspoonful of the roasted garlic puree and the croutons and serve. **SERVES 6**

Thin French bread croutons, for garnish (p. 52)

creamy cauliflower soup

½ medium-size head
   cauliflower, separated
   into 1-inch florets

3 tablespoons butter

¾ pound russet (baking)
   potatoes, peeled &
   thinly sliced

2 cups chicken stock
   (p. 70), broth or
   vegetable stock (p. 77)

2 cups milk

Salt & freshly ground
   pepper

1 large carrot, cut into
   julienne

1 large leek (white part
   only), halved lengthwise,
   cut into julienne &
   washed well

1 large celery stalk,
   peeled & cut into
   julienne

2 tablespoons chopped
   fresh chervil or parsley

Cutting vegetables into julienne strips takes time and patience, but the elegant look they lend the soup makes it worth the effort.

Bring a large saucepan of salted water to a boil. Add the cauliflower and boil for 2 minutes, or until crisp-tender. Using a slotted spoon, transfer the cauliflower to a bowl and set aside.

In a large heavy pot, melt the butter over medium-high heat. Add the potatoes and reduce the heat to medium. Cover and cook, stirring, for 15 minutes, or until the potatoes are soft. Add the cauliflower, stock, and milk, and season with salt and pepper. Cover and cook for 15 minutes, or until the vegetables are soft. In a food processor or blender, puree the soup in batches. Return the soup to the pot and reheat.

Meanwhile, put the carrot, leek, and celery into the boiling water and cook for 3 minutes, or until tender. Drain and rinse under cold water. Set aside a small amount for garnish.

Stir the remaining vegetables into the soup. Serve, garnished with the vegetables and chervil. **SERVES 4 TO 6**

summer tomato, corn & okra soup

For an authentic South Carolina version of this chunky soup, add half a cup of raw rice to the onions instead of the corn, omit the flour, and cook the soup for twenty minutes before adding the okra.

In a large nonreactive pot, heat the oil over medium-high heat. Add the onion and cook, stirring often, for about 3 minutes, or until softened. Add the corn and cook for 2 minutes, or until heated through. Sprinkle with the flour and cook, stirring, for 3 to 5 minutes, until the flour is lightly browned. Add the tomatoes and cook, scraping the bottom of the pan, for 3 minutes, or until the juices have thickened.

Add the stock to the pan, increase the heat to high, and bring to a boil.

Add the okra and reduce the heat to low. Cook, uncovered, for 5 to 7 minutes, until the okra is tender. Season with salt and pepper, ladle the soup into deep bowls, and serve.

SERVES 6

2 tablespoons olive oil

1 large onion, chopped

2 cups fresh corn kernels (from about 3 ears)

2 tablespoons all-purpose flour

1½ pounds tomatoes, seeded & chopped

4 cups chicken stock (p. 70) or broth

½ pound okra, cut into ¼-inch-thick slices

Salt & freshly ground pepper

gazpacho

3 pounds tomatoes,
   peeled, seeded &
   coarsely chopped

1 large green bell pepper,
   halved, cored, seeded
   & chopped

1 cucumber, peeled,
   seeded & chopped

1 small onion, finely
   chopped

1 small garlic clove,
   minced

1 cup chilled tomato juice

¼ cup red wine vinegar

2 tablespoons olive oil

Salt & freshly ground
   pepper

Diced cucumber, green
   pepper, tomatoes
   & onion, for garnish

Chunky French bread
   croutons, for garnish
   (p. 52)

In this, my favorite gazpacho, the vegetable base is pureed, making it especially light and flavorful. The soup is finished off with a generous topping of diced vegetables and crisp homemade croutons.

In a food processor or blender, puree the tomatoes, bell pepper, cucumber, onion, and garlic, in batches.

Transfer the puree to a large bowl and stir in the tomato juice, vinegar, and oil. Season with salt and pepper. Pour the soup through a strainer set over a large bowl; discard the solids. Cover and refrigerate several hours or overnight.

To serve, divide the soup among small chilled bowls and top with the diced vegetables and croutons.   **SERVES 4**

tomato-eggplant soup with roasted peppers

1 medium-size eggplant, peeled & cut into 1-inch cubes

2 tablespoons fresh lemon juice

Salt

2 tablespoons olive oil

1 large onion, chopped

1 garlic clove, minced

1½ pounds tomatoes, peeled, seeded & chopped

1 tablespoon chopped fresh thyme

Freshly ground pepper

1 each red & yellow bell pepper, roasted, peeled, cored & seeded (p. 25)

2 cups vegetable stock (p. 77) or broth

1 tablespoon chopped fresh parsley

Sprinkling the eggplant with salt will draw out the bitter juices, letting the eggplant impart a delicate smoky flavor to the soup.

Put the eggplant into a colander and sprinkle with the lemon juice and 2 teaspoons salt. Toss and set aside for 30 minutes.

In a large nonreactive pot, heat the oil over medium heat. Add the onion and cook for 3 minutes, or until softened. Add the garlic and cook for 1 minute. Add the tomatoes and thyme.

Rinse the eggplant and pat dry. Add to the pot, and season with salt and pepper. Cover and cook over medium heat, stirring, for 10 minutes, or until the eggplant is very soft.

Meanwhile, cut half of the roasted peppers into small dice and set aside for garnish. Chop the remaining peppers and add to the pot. Pour in the stock, increase the heat to high, and bring to a boil. Reduce the heat to medium, cover, and cook for 5 minutes. In a blender, puree the soup in batches. Season with salt and pepper, stir in the parsley, and reheat. Serve garnished with the diced peppers. **SERVES 4**

root vegetable soup with caramelized onions

Roasting root vegetables brings out their sweet flavor, adding interest and depth of flavor.

Preheat the oven to 350°F. In a large roasting pan, put the celery root, potatoes, parsnips, and carrots. Drizzle with the oil and season with salt and pepper. Add the tomato and roast the vegetables, stirring, for 1½ to 2 hours, until tender.

Meanwhile, prepare the caramelized onions: In a heavy medium-size skillet, melt the butter over medium-high heat. Add the onion, sugar, salt, and pepper and cook, stirring, for 15 minutes, or until the onions are deep brown. Set aside.

Pour 1 cup of the stock into the roasting pan, scraping to loosen any browned bits. Transfer the vegetables and liquid to a large nonreactive pot and stir in the remaining stock. Bring to a boil. Cook for 10 minutes, or until the vegetables are soft.

In a food processor or blender, puree the soup in batches. Return the soup to the pot, season to taste with salt and pepper if necessary, and reheat. Ladle into large bowls and garnish with the caramelized onions. **SERVES 6**

1 pound each celery root & all-purpose potatoes, peeled & cut into chunks

2 each medium-size parsnips & carrots, peeled & cut into 1½-inch pieces

2 tablespoons olive oil

Salt & freshly ground pepper

1 large tomato, quartered

CARAMELIZED ONIONS

1 tablespoon butter

1 large onion, thinly sliced

1 teaspoon sugar

½ teaspoon each salt & freshly ground pepper

6 cups vegetable stock (p. 77) or broth

split pea soup with garlic croutons

**2 tablespoons
unsalted butter**

**2 tablespoons
vegetable oil**

2 garlic cloves, crushed

**3 to 4 thick slices day-old
white bread, crusts
removed & cut into
½-inch cubes**

1 smoked ham hock

**2 tablespoons vegetable
oil**

2 carrots, finely chopped

1 onion, finely chopped

**1 celery stalk, finely
chopped**

**1 pound green split peas,
picked over & rinsed**

**6 cups chicken stock
(p. 70) or broth, plus
additional if needed**

*The aroma of smoked ham hock simmering
with split peas will warm even the coldest
winter kitchen.*

Prepare the garlic croutons: In a small skillet, melt the butter
with the oil over medium heat. Add the garlic and bread cubes.
Cook, stirring often, for 5 to 7 minutes, until the croutons are
golden brown and fragrant. Transfer the croutons to a paper
towel–lined plate and set aside.

Put the ham hock into a large saucepan and add enough
cold water to cover. Bring to a boil over high heat, reduce the
heat to medium, and simmer for 10 minutes. Drain and rinse
under cold running water.

In a large pot, heat the oil over medium-high heat. Add the
carrots, onion, and celery. Cook, stirring often, for 5 minutes,
or until the onion is softened. Add the split peas and cook for
2 minutes longer. Add the ham hock and stock and season with
salt and pepper. Increase the heat to high and bring to a boil.
Reduce the heat and simmer, partially covered, stirring often,

Salt & freshly ground pepper

½ cup heavy cream

for 45 minutes to 1 hour, until the split peas are very tender, adding additional stock if the soup seems too thick. Transfer the ham hock to a plate and set aside.

In a food processor or blender, puree the soup in batches. Pour the soup through a strainer set over a large bowl, pressing hard on the solids with the back of a spoon to extract as much liquid as possible.

When cool enough to handle, remove all the lean pieces of ham and finely dice them.

Put the soup and cream into a large saucepan, season with salt and pepper if necessary, and reheat. Ladle the soup into bowls and top with the diced ham and garlic croutons.

SERVES 4

potato, cabbage & bacon soup

Yukon Gold potatoes, readily available in supermarkets, are ideal for this classic winter soup. They hold their shape well and have a rich buttery flavor and deep golden color.

Cook the bacon in a large nonreactive pot over medium heat until crisp and browned. Transfer the bacon to a paper towel–lined plate. Discard all but 1 tablespoon of the fat.

Add the onion to the pot and cook, stirring, for 3 minutes, or until softened. Add the potatoes and cabbage and cook, stirring, for 5 to 7 minutes, until the potatoes are slightly softened and the cabbage is wilted. Add the vinegar and cook, stirring, for 2 minutes, or until the vinegar has evaporated. Pour in the stock, season with salt and pepper, and bring to a boil over high heat. Reduce the heat to medium and simmer for 30 minutes, or until the potatoes and cabbage are very tender.

Add the bacon to the soup, stir in the caraway seeds, and season to taste with salt and pepper if necessary. Ladle into large bowls and sprinkle with the parsley.   **SERVES 4**

¼ pound bacon, coarsely chopped

1 large onion, finely chopped

2 pounds potatoes, preferably Yukon Gold, peeled & cut into ½-inch cubes

½ small head green cabbage, finely shredded

¼ cup red wine vinegar

6 cups chicken stock (p. 70) or broth

Salt & freshly ground pepper

1 tablespoon caraway seeds

1 tablespoon finely chopped fresh parsley

lentil soup with sausages

1 smoked ham hock

2 tablespoons vegetable oil

2 carrots, chopped

1 onion, chopped

1 celery stalk, chopped

½ pound lentils (about 1¼ cups), preferably lentils de Puy, picked over & rinsed *(see Note)*

2 garlic cloves, minced

Cold water

Salt & freshly ground pepper

1 pound mild or hot Italian sausage

2 tablespoons olive oil

Lentils de Puy, the preferable variety here, come from the town of Le Puy in France. They are smaller and firmer than other lentils and have a deep, earthy flavor that makes them worth seeking out.

Place the ham hock in a large saucepan and add enough cold water to cover. Bring to a boil over high heat, reduce the heat to medium, and simmer for 10 minutes. Drain and rinse the ham hock under cold running water.

Meanwhile, in a large heavy pot, heat the vegetable oil over medium-high heat. Add the carrots, onion, and celery. Cook, stirring, for 5 to 7 minutes, until the onion is softened.

Add the ham hock, lentils, and garlic to the pot and pour in enough cold water to cover the ham hock by 2 inches. Bring to a boil over high heat. Reduce the heat to medium and simmer, stirring occasionally, for 30 to 45 minutes, until the lentils are tender, adding additional water to keep the lentils covered with water by about 1 inch. Discard the ham hock and season the soup to taste with salt and pepper if necessary.

Meanwhile, prick the sausages with a fork. Place in a small skillet and add enough cold water to cover. Cook over medium-high heat for 6 to 7 minutes, until firm to the touch. Remove the sausages to a plate. Pour off any water from the skillet and wipe the skillet clean. Add the olive oil to the skillet along with the sausages and cook over medium heat, turning them often, for 7 to 10 minutes, until well browned. Transfer to a paper towel–lined plate.

In a food processor or blender, puree the soup in batches. Return the puree to the pot. Reheat the soup, thinning it with water if needed. Season the soup to taste with salt and pepper if necessary.

Cut the sausages into $1/4$-inch-thick slices and place in the bottom of deep bowls. Ladle the hot soup over and serve.

SERVES 4

NOTE

Lentils de Puy are available in specialty food stores and by mail order.

bean & bacon soup

1 pound dried Great Northern beans, picked over & rinsed

1 fresh rosemary sprig

1 bay leaf

10 whole black peppercorns

Salt

¼ pound slab bacon, cut into ¼-inch dice

2 carrots, chopped

1 large onion, chopped

1 celery stalk, chopped

1 large tomato, seeded & chopped

4 cups chicken stock (p. 70) or broth

Freshly ground pepper

Diced pieces of smoky bacon make a toothsome garnish for this stick-to-your-ribs soup, but chopped, thick-sliced, or regular bacon will work just fine.

In a large bowl, soak the beans overnight in water to cover by 3 inches. Drain.

In a large saucepan, combine the beans with enough water to cover by 3 inches. Make a bouquet garni: Put the rosemary, bay leaf, and peppercorns on a small piece of cheesecloth, tie with kitchen string, and put into the pot. Bring to a boil over medium-high heat, skimming off any froth that rises to the surface. Reduce the heat to medium-low, partially cover, and simmer for 1 hour, or until the beans are just tender.

Remove from the heat and stir in 2 teaspoons salt. Cover and set aside for 30 minutes.

Meanwhile, cook the bacon in a large pot over medium heat until crisp and browned. Using a slotted spoon, transfer the bacon to a paper towel–lined plate to drain.

Pour off all but 1 tablespoon of the fat from the pot. Add the carrots, onion, and celery to the pot. Cook over medium-high heat, stirring often, for 3 to 5 minutes, until the onion is softened. Add the tomato and cook for 2 minutes.

Drain the beans, discarding the bouquet garni, and add to the vegetables. Pour in the stock, increase the heat to high, and bring to a boil. Reduce the heat to medium. Cover and cook for 10 minutes, or until the flavors have blended.

In a food processor or blender, puree the soup in batches. Pour the puree through a strainer set over a large saucepan.

Bring the soup to a simmer over medium heat and season with salt and pepper. Ladle into large bowls and sprinkle with the bacon.   **SERVES 6**

hearty chicken & portobello mushroom soup

This is a substantial main-dish soup, just right for a late Sunday supper. Use an assortment of exotic wild mushrooms, such as cremini, wood ear, or lobster in place of the portobellos for an exotic touch.

Place the chicken in a large pot. Add the carrots, onion, and celery, and enough cold water to cover. Season with salt and pepper and bring to a boil over high heat. Reduce the heat to medium-low and simmer, uncovered, for 1½ to 2 hours, until the chicken meat is falling off the bones.

Remove the chicken to a platter. Pour the broth through a strainer set over a large bowl, discarding the vegetables. Measure and set aside 6 cups of the broth. (Refrigerate or freeze any extra broth for another use.)

When the chicken is cool enough to handle, remove the meat from the bones and discard the skin, bones, and gristle. Cut the chicken into 1½-inch chunks and put into a bowl.

1 (3½ to 4 pound) chicken

2 carrots, coarsely chopped

1 medium-size onion, quartered

1 celery stalk, coarsely chopped

About 10 cups cold water

Salt & freshly ground pepper

3 small portobello mushrooms, stems removed & cleaned

20 small asparagus tips, about 1½ inches long (reserve stalks for another use)

3 tablespoons unsalted butter

3 tablespoons all-purpose flour

1 cup frozen mixed carrots & peas, thawed

1 tablespoon chopped fresh parsley

Meanwhile, preheat the oven to 350°F. Place the mushrooms on a baking sheet and season with salt and pepper. Bake for 20 to 30 minutes, until lightly browned and soft to the touch. Transfer to a paper towel–lined plate to drain, then cut into ¼-inch-thick slices. Set aside.

Bring a medium-size saucepan of salted water to a boil. Add the asparagus tips, bring the water back to a boil, and cook for 2 to 3 minutes, until slightly softened. Drain, rinse under cold running water, and drain on a paper towel–lined plate.

Melt the butter in a large pot. Add the flour and cook over medium-high heat, whisking, for 3 minutes, or until golden. Whisk in the reserved broth and increase the heat to high. Bring to a boil and cook, stirring often, for 10 minutes, or until slightly thickened. Reduce the heat to medium and season with salt and pepper. Stir in the chicken, mushrooms, asparagus tips, and the peas and carrots. Season to taste with salt and pepper if necessary and cook for about 5 minutes longer, or until heated through. Ladle into large bowls and garnish with the chopped parsley. **SERVES 6**

beef & barley soup

For the best results in this ideal wintertime soup, use a cut of beef that benefits from long, slow cooking, such as shank or chuck.

In a large pot, heat $1\frac{1}{2}$ tablespoons of the oil over medium-high heat. Add half the leeks, onions, carrots, and celery and cook, stirring often, for about 5 minutes, or until the onion is softened. (Put the remaining vegetables into a bowl, cover with plastic wrap, and refrigerate.)

Season the beef on both sides with salt and pepper and place on top of the vegetables. Pour in the water, cover, and bring to a boil. Reduce the heat and gently simmer, partially covered, for 3 to 4 hours, until the beef shreds easily with two forks. Check the liquid in the pot occasionally, adding cold water to cover the beef if needed.

Transfer the beef to a cutting board and cover loosely. Pour the cooking broth through a strainer set over a large bowl, pressing on the solids to extract as much liquid as possible. Skim off the fat and measure the broth. You should have about 4

3 tablespoons olive oil

2 medium-size leeks (white part only), thinly sliced & washed well

2 onions, chopped

2 carrots, chopped

2 celery stalks, thinly sliced

Two $1\frac{1}{2}$-inch-thick pieces beef shank (about $1\frac{1}{2}$ pounds each)

Salt & freshly ground pepper

6 cups cold water

Beef broth (optional)

$\frac{1}{2}$ cup pearl barley

cups. If not, add enough water or beef broth to equal this amount and set aside. (If you have any extra broth, refrigerate or freeze for another use.)

In a large pot, heat the remaining 1½ tablespoons oil over medium-high heat. Add the reserved leeks, onions, carrots, and celery. Cook, stirring often, for about 3 minutes, or until slightly softened. Stir in the barley and cook for 3 to 5 minutes. Pour in the broth and bring to a boil. Season with salt and pepper. Cover, reduce the heat to medium, and simmer for about 30 minutes, or until the barley is tender.

Meanwhile, trim the beef of all fat and gristle and discard the bones. Cut the beef into ½-inch chunks. Add the beef to the soup. Simmer, partially covered, for 10 to 15 minutes, until the beef is heated through and the barley is very soft. Season to taste with salt and pepper if necessary and serve in large bowls. **SERVES 4**

lemon chicken soup with herb dumplings

HERB DUMPLINGS

1 cup all-purpose flour

1½ teaspoons baking powder

½ teaspoon salt

2 tablespoons unsalted butter, cut into small pieces

¼ cup milk

1 large egg, lightly beaten

2 tablespoons mixed chopped fresh herbs, such as thyme, parsley, oregano & basil

CHICKEN SOUP

1 (4 to 5 pound) chicken

2 carrots, coarsely chopped

1 onion, quartered

1 celery stalk, coarsely chopped

Chilling the herb dough for about thirty minutes makes it easier to shape the dumplings for this comforting cold-weather soup.

Prepare the herb dumplings: In a medium-size bowl, mix the flour, baking powder, and salt. With a pastry blender or two forks, cut in the butter until the mixture forms a coarse meal. In a small bowl, combine the milk, egg, and herbs. Pour over the flour mixture and stir with a fork until the dough pulls away from the sides of the bowl; do not overwork. Cover with plastic wrap and refrigerate for 30 minutes.

With floured hands, lightly shape the dough into 24 walnut-size balls. Place the dumplings on a plate and chill for at least 30 minutes, or up to several hours.

Meanwhile, prepare the chicken soup: Place the chicken in a large pot. Add the carrots, onion, celery, thyme, bay leaf, and enough cold water to cover. Season with salt and pepper. Bring to a boil over high heat. Reduce the heat to medium-low and simmer, uncovered, for 1½ to 2 hours, until the chicken is falling off the bones. Transfer the chicken to a platter. When the chicken is cool enough to handle, remove the meat from the bones and discard the skin, bones, and gristle. Cut the chicken into large chunks and set aside.

Meanwhile, pour the broth through a strainer set over a large bowl; discard the solids. You should have about 5 cups broth; set aside. If necessary, add water to equal 5 cups.

Melt the butter in a large nonreactive pot. Add the flour and cook over medium-high heat, stirring, for 3 minutes, or until bubbling smooth. Whisk in the broth, increase the heat to high, and bring to a boil. Cook, whisking, for 10 minutes, or until the broth is slightly thickened. Reduce the heat to medium and season well with salt and pepper. Stir in the cream, lemon zest and juice, and the chicken.

Drop the dumplings into the simmering soup. Cover and cook, stirring occasionally, for 15 minutes, or until the dumplings are puffed and cooked through. Ladle the soup and dumplings into large shallow bowls and serve. **SERVES 6**

2 fresh thyme sprigs

1 bay leaf

Cold water

Salt & freshly ground pepper

3 tablespoons unsalted butter

3 tablespoons all-purpose flour

½ cup heavy cream

Grated zest of 1 lemon

Juice of 1 lemon

4 dozen soft-shell clams (steamers), scrubbed
(*see Note*)

1 cup cold water

¼ pound salt pork, cut into ¼-inch dice
(*see Note*)

1 medium-size onion, chopped

1 celery stalk, peeled & thinly sliced

2 large all-purpose potatoes (about 1½ pounds), peeled & cut into ½-inch dice

2 cups fish stock (p. 73) or water

4 cups milk

Salt & freshly ground pepper

2 tablespoons unsalted butter, cut into small pieces

For the best results in this ever popular seafood chowder, take care not to overcook the clams or they will be tough. And for a classic presentation, serve it accompanied by oyster or soda crackers.

In a large pot, combine the clams and water. Bring to a boil over high heat, cover, and reduce the heat to medium. Steam the clams for 10 minutes, or until they have opened. Discard any that do not open. Working over a bowl, shuck the clams. Pull off and discard the black sheath that covers the "tails" and separate the clam bellies from the tails. Transfer the clam bellies to a medium-size bowl; cover and refrigerate. Finely chop the tails, put into a small dish, and refrigerate. Line a strainer with a double thickness of dampened cheesecloth, set over a medium-size bowl, and pour the clam liquid through. Set the clam liquid aside.

In a large heavy saucepan, cook the salt pork over medium-high heat for 2 to 3 minutes, until it begins to render its fat.

Add the onion and celery and cook, stirring often, for 3 to 5 minutes, until the onion is softened. Add the potatoes and clam tails. Pour in the fish stock, increase the heat to high, and bring to a boil. Reduce the heat to medium and simmer for about 15 minutes, until the potatoes are tender.

Add the clam bellies and the reserved clam liquid to the soup and heat until bubbles form around the edge. Stir in the milk and bring to a simmer. Season to taste with salt and pepper and float the butter on top. Ladle the soup into bowls and sprinkle with the parsley. **SERVES 6**

1 tablespoon chopped fresh parsley

NOTE

If soft-shell clams aren't available, use the large quahog clams and omit the "tail" prep.

Salt pork can be found in the meat department of supermarkets.

mediterranean fish soup

AÏOLI

6 garlic cloves

Salt

1 large egg yolk

½ cup vegetable oil

½ cup olive oil

Several drops of Tabasco

Freshly ground pepper

CROUTONS

2 tablespoons unsalted butter

2 tablespoons vegetable oil

12 to 15 thin slices day-old French baguette

3 tablespoons unsalted butter

1 large onion, thinly sliced

For true authenticity, spread a little aïoli on each crouton and place on top of the soup. The intense, creamy garlic sauce will melt into the broth, enlivening the flavor.

Prepare the aïoli: With a mortar and pestle, pound the garlic with ½ teaspoon salt until it forms a thick paste. Transfer to a bowl, whisk in the egg yolk, then drizzle in 2 tablespoons of the vegetable oil, whisking constantly. Add the remaining 6 tablespoons vegetable oil and the olive oil in a slow steady stream, whisking constantly until the mixture is the consistency of thick mayonnaise. Add the Tabasco and season the aïoli with additional salt and pepper if necessary. Cover with plastic wrap and refrigerate until ready to use.

Prepare the croutons: In a large skillet, melt the butter with the oil over medium-high heat. Add the bread and cook, turning often, for 2 to 3 minutes, until golden brown. Transfer to a paper towel–lined plate and set aside.

In a large heavy pot, melt the butter over medium-high

1 celery stalk, peeled
  & cut into fine julienne

1 large fennel bulb,
  trimmed & thinly sliced,
  feathery tops reserved

1 medium-size leek (white
  part only), halved
  lengthwise, cut into
  julienne & washed well

3 cups fish stock (p. 73)

1 pound tomatoes,
  peeled, seeded &
  chopped

Pinch of saffron threads

Salt & freshly ground
  pepper

2½ to 3 pounds lean
  white fish fillets, such
  as sea bass, monkfish,
  whiting, snapper,
  or cod, cut into large
  chunks

heat. Add the onion, celery, fennel, and leek. Cook, stirring often, for 5 to 7 minutes, until softened. Add the fish stock and bring to a boil. Reduce the heat to medium-low, stir in the tomatoes and saffron, and season with salt and pepper. Simmer, stirring occasionally, for about 10 minutes, or until the flavors have blended.

Add the fish and cook for about 10 minutes, or until opaque throughout. Season the soup to taste with salt and pepper if necessary. Using a slotted spoon, place the fish in large shallow bowls, ladle in the soup, and top with the aïoli and croutons.   **SERVES 6**

meatball soup with rice

The savory lamb meatballs are a perfect partner for the clean-tasting broth. They can be prepared ahead and frozen for up to a month. Simply thaw them in the refrigerator before adding them to the soup.

Prepare the lamb meatballs: In a small skillet, heat the oil over medium-high heat. Add the onion and celery and cook, stirring often, for 3 minutes, or until the onion is softened. Add the garlic and cook for 1 minute longer, until fragrant. Remove from the heat and let cool.

In a large bowl, combine the lamb, bread crumbs, egg, salt, and pepper. Add the cooled onion mixture and stir until well blended. Cover with plastic wrap and refrigerate for at least 2 hours. (The meatball mixture can be prepared up to 1 day in advance.)

Using a melon baller or measuring teaspoon, roll about 60 olive-size meatballs. Place the meatballs on a large plate, cover with plastic wrap, and refrigerate.

LAMB MEATBALLS

2 tablespoons olive oil

1 small onion, finely chopped

1 celery stalk, finely chopped

1 garlic clove, minced

¾ pound ground lamb

1 cup fresh bread crumbs

1 large egg, lightly beaten

1 teaspoon salt

½ teaspoon freshly ground pepper

2 tablespoons butter

½ cup long-grain rice

8 cups chicken stock (p. 70) or broth

2 carrots, cut into ½-inch cubes

1 cup tiny broccoli florets

In a large pot, melt the butter over medium-high heat. Add the rice and cook, stirring, for about 2 minutes, or until translucent. Pour in the stock, increase the heat to high, and bring to a boil. Reduce the heat to medium-low, cover, and cook for 15 minutes, or until the rice is tender.

Meanwhile, bring a large saucepan of salted water to a boil over high heat. Add the carrots and cook for 3 to 4 minutes, or until barely tender. Using a slotted spoon, transfer the carrots to a colander and cool under cold running water. Add the broccoli to the saucepan. As soon as the water returns to a boil, transfer the broccoli to the colander with the carrots and cool under cold running water. Set aside.

Add the meatballs to the broth, reduce the heat to medium, and cook for about 10 minutes, or until the meatballs are no longer pink. Add the carrots and broccoli, cover, and cook for 5 minutes longer, or until heated through. Season the soup with salt and pepper, stir in the parsley, and ladle into large bowls. **SERVES 6**

Salt & freshly ground pepper

1 tablespoon finely chopped fresh parsley

duck wonton soup

1 (2 to 2½ pound) duck,
  excess fat removed

2 carrots, cut into
  2-inch chunks

1 large onion, quartered

1 celery stalk, cut into
  2-inch lengths

Cold water

Chicken stock (p. 70) or
  broth

DUCK WONTONS

2 tablespoons butter

2 large shallots, minced

2 tablespoons dry sherry

2 teaspoons grated peeled
  fresh ginger

1 tablespoon soy sauce

Salt & freshly ground
  pepper

This is a surprisingly light soup that makes an ideal first course for a fall or winter meal. Begin the preparation a day ahead to facilitate the removal of the fat from the duck broth.

In a large pot, put the duck, carrots, onion, and celery. Pour in enough cold water to cover by 1 inch and bring to a simmer over high heat. Reduce the heat to medium-low and simmer for 2 to 2½ hours, until the meat is falling off the bone, occasionally skimming off any froth that rises to the surface.

Transfer the duck to a platter and refrigerate. Pour the duck broth through a strainer set over a large bowl, discarding the vegetables. Refrigerate the broth until well chilled.

Remove the layer of fat from the broth and measure the broth. You should have about 6 cups. If you have more, boil the broth until reduced to 6 cups. If you have less, add enough chicken stock to equal this amount.

Remove the meat from the duck, discarding the skin, bones, and gristle. Finely chop the duck meat.

Prepare the duck wontons: Melt the butter in a small skillet over medium heat. Add the shallots and cook, stirring, for 2 minutes, or until softened but not browned. Transfer to a large bowl, add the duck, sherry, ginger, and soy sauce, and season with salt and pepper, tossing to combine.

Place a wonton wrapper on a work surface, with one corner facing you. Place 1 teaspoonful of the duck mixture in the lower center of the wrapper. Brush the edges with a little water and fold the top half of the wrapper over the filling to form a triangle. Firmly press the edges to seal. Continue filling and shaping the wontons. (Save the leftover filling for another use, or make additional wontons and freeze.)

In a large pot, bring the duck broth to a boil, then reduce the heat to medium. Add the scallions, bell pepper, and wontons and cook for 10 minutes, or until the wontons are cooked through and the peppers have softened. Season to taste with salt and pepper if necessary. Using a slotted spoon, transfer the wontons to large shallow bowls and ladle the hot broth over.

SERVES 4

24 wonton wrappers
(see Note)

4 slender scallions, thinly sliced

½ red bell pepper, cored, seeded & cut into ¼-inch dice

Salt & freshly ground pepper

NOTE

Wonton wrappers are available in the Asian food section of large grocery stores and in Asian markets.

oxtail soup

OXTAIL BROTH

4 pounds oxtails, cut into 1-inch pieces & trimmed of excess fat (*see Note*)

2 medium-size leeks (white part only), thinly sliced & washed well

2 carrots, cut into large chunks

1 onion, quartered

1 celery stalk, cut into large chunks

Cold water

1 bay leaf

12 whole black peppercorns

Salt

1 pound all-purpose potatoes, peeled & cut into ½-inch cubes

If you have only sampled the canned variety, you are in for a real treat. Homemade oxtail soup is rich and full-bodied with a satisfying unctuous quality, making it welcome cold-weather fare.

Prepare the oxtail broth: In a large pot, put the oxtails, leeks, carrots, onion, and celery. Pour in enough cold water to cover by 2 inches. Add the bay leaf and peppercorns, season with salt, and bring to a boil over high heat. Reduce the heat to medium-low and simmer for 3 hours, or until the oxtails are very tender, skimming off any froth that rises to the surface. Add additional water if necessary to keep the oxtails covered by 1 inch.

Transfer the oxtails to a plate. Pour the oxtail broth through a strainer set over a large bowl, discarding the solids. Refrigerate the broth for at least 8 hours or until chilled.

When the oxtails are cool enough to handle, remove the meat, discarding the fat, bones, and gristle. Put the meat on a plate, cover with plastic wrap, and refrigerate.

Put the potatoes into a large pot. Add enough cold water to cover, salt the water, and bring to a boil. Cook the potatoes for 10 to 15 minutes, until tender. Using a slotted spoon, remove the potatoes to a large bowl. Add the carrots to the boiling water and cook for 7 to 10 minutes, until tender. Using a slotted spoon, transfer to a colander, rinse under cold running water, and add to the potatoes. Add the leeks to the boiling water and boil rapidly for 1 minute. Drain, rinse under cold running water, and add to the vegetables.

Remove the fat from the broth and measure the broth. You should have about 6 cups. If you have more, boil the broth until reduced to 6 cups. If you have less, add enough beef broth to equal 6 cups.

To serve, in a large pot, heat the broth over medium-high heat. Add the reserved oxtail meat and the vegetables and bring to a boil. Season with salt and pepper and ladle into large bowls. **SERVES 4 TO 6**

2 carrots, cut into ½-inch cubes

1 medium-size leek (white part only), halved lengthwise, thinly sliced & washed well

Beef broth

Salt & freshly ground pepper

N O T E

Oxtails are available in butcher shops and in most supermarkets.

black bean soup with pork & fresh chiles

1 pound dried black beans, picked over & rinsed

MARINATED PORK

¾ pound boneless pork loin or pork tenderloin, cut into 1-inch cubes

2 teaspoons pure chile powder

1 teaspoon ground cumin

¼ teaspoon salt

½ teaspoon freshly ground pepper

3 tablespoons vegetable oil

2 carrots, chopped

1 large onion, chopped

1 celery stalk, chopped

1 garlic clove, minced

Few foods are more inviting than a fragrant bowl of black bean soup. My version, a fusion of Caribbean and Southwest flavors, becomes a meal with the addition of chile-marinated pork.

In a large bowl, soak the beans overnight in water to cover by 3 inches. Drain and set aside.

Meanwhile, prepare the marinated pork: In a large bowl, toss the pork with the chile powder, cumin, salt, and pepper. Cover and refrigerate for at least 6 hours or overnight, tossing the pork occasionally.

In a large pot, heat 1 tablespoon of the oil over medium-high heat. Add the carrots, onion, and celery and cook for 3 to 5 minutes, until softened. Add the garlic and cook for 1 minute longer. Stir in the beans and add enough water to cover by 1 inch. Increase the heat to high and bring to a boil. Reduce the heat to medium and simmer, partially covered, for 1½ to 2 hours, until the beans are tender; season with salt during the last 30 minutes.

In a food processor or blender, puree the soup in batches, adding water if the soup seems too thick. Transfer to a large saucepan, add the sherry, and season to taste with salt and pepper if necessary. Keep warm over low heat.

In a medium-size skillet, heat the remaining 2 tablespoons oil over medium-high heat. Pat the pork dry and cook, turning often, for about 10 minutes, or until cooked through.

Divide the pork among soup bowls, ladle in the soup, and garnish with the chiles. **SERVES 6**

¼ cup dry sherry

Salt & freshly ground pepper

2 poblano chiles, roasted, peeled, cored, seeded & cut into ¼-inch dice

NOTE

To prepare the chiles, preheat the broiler to high. Broil the chiles for 3 to 4 minutes, or until the skin is blistered and brown. Wrap the chiles in a paper towel, seal tightly in a plastic bag, and steam for 10 minutes. Remove the chiles and let cool, then peel, core and seed.

minestrone

This is my favorite rendition of a much-loved soup that has endless variations. Feel free to use other vegetables that look especially fresh or are the pick of the season.

In a large nonreactive pot, heat the oil over medium-high heat. Add the carrots, onion, celery, and garlic. Cook, stirring often, for 3 to 5 minutes, until the onion is softened. Stir in the tomatoes and cook for 2 minutes. Pour in the stock, increase the heat to high, and bring to a boil. Reduce the heat to medium and simmer, stirring often, for 10 minutes, or until reduced.

Meanwhile, bring a large saucepan of salted water to a boil. Add the cauliflower, zucchini, and green beans. As soon as the water returns to a boil, drain the vegetables.

Stir the cauliflower, zucchini, green beans, and cannellini beans into the soup; season with salt and pepper. Simmer for 10 minutes, or until the vegetables are just tender. Stir in the basil and ladle into bowls, passing the Parmesan separately.

SERVES 4 TO 6

2 tablespoons olive oil

2 carrots, chopped

1 onion, chopped

2 celery stalks, chopped

1 garlic clove, minced

1 pound tomatoes, seeded & chopped

6 cups chicken broth

1 cup small cauliflower florets

1 large zucchini, cut into ½-inch cubes

¼ pound slender green beans, trimmed & cut into ¼-inch pieces

1 cup cooked cannellini beans

Salt & freshly ground pepper

2 tablespoons chopped fresh basil

Freshly grated Parmesan cheese, for serving

2 tablespoons unsalted butter

1 medium-size onion, finely chopped

2 celery stalks, thinly sliced

6 pounds small mussels, scrubbed well & debearded

1 cup dry white wine

Pinch of saffron threads, soaked in 1 teaspoon hot water

About 3 cups heavy cream

Salt & freshly ground pepper

In this unusual French mussel soup, the enticing briny flavor is derived from the cooking liquid; most of the mussels are set aside. Use them for mussels rémoulade or cold mussels with watercress mayonnaise.

In a large nonreactive pot, melt the butter over medium-high heat. Add the onion and celery and cook, stirring, for 5 minutes, or until the onion is softened. Add the mussels, wine, and the saffron with its liquid. Cook, covered, for 7 minutes, or until the mussels have opened. Discard any that do not open.

With a slotted spoon, transfer the mussels to a large bowl. Remove the mussels from their shells. Reserve one third of the mussels for garnish; refrigerate the remainder for another use.

Line a strainer with cheesecloth, set over a large bowl, and pour the mussel liquid through. Measure and add enough cream to equal 4 cups. Pour into a large saucepan, season with salt and pepper, and reheat, but do not let boil. Ladle into small bowls and garnish with the reserved mussels. **SERVES 4**

If you happen to have a piece of Parmesan cheese rind on hand, by all means add it. It will add richness and depth of flavor to this comforting pasta and bean soup.

In a large bowl, soak the beans overnight in water to cover by 3 inches. Drain.

In a large saucepan, combine the beans with enough water to cover by 3 inches. Bring to a boil over medium-high heat, skimming off any froth that rises to the surface. Reduce the heat, partially cover, and simmer for about 1 hour, or until the beans are tender. Stir in 2 teaspoons salt, remove from the heat, and cover. Set aside.

In a large pot, heat the oil over medium-high heat. Add the carrots, onion, and celery and cook, stirring, for 3 to 5 minutes, until the onion is softened. Stir in the beans, tomato, and stock and bring to a boil. Add the pasta and simmer, covered, for 10 to 15 minutes, until the pasta is tender. Season to taste with salt and pepper and serve. **SERVES 6**

1 pound dried navy beans, picked over & rinsed

Salt

2 tablespoons olive oil

2 carrots, chopped

1 large onion, chopped

1 celery stalk, chopped

1 large tomato, peeled, seeded & chopped

6 cups chicken stock (p. 70) or broth

½ cup small elbow macaroni

Freshly ground pepper

portuguese kale soup with linguiça

¾ **pound kale, tough stems removed & washed well**

1¼ **pounds all-purpose potatoes, peeled & cut into ½-inch cubes**

½ **pound linguiça or spicy Italian sausage, pierced with a fork** *(see Note)*

2 **small garlic cloves, crushed**

3 **cups chicken stock** *(recipe follows)* **or broth**

Salt & freshly ground pepper

½ **red bell pepper, cored, seeded & very thinly sliced**

Kale soup, caldo verde, *is the national soup of Portugal and can be found on just about every restaurant menu. If you prefer, spinach makes a fine substitute for the kale and takes a little less time to cook.*

Bring a large pot of salted water to a boil over high heat. Stack the kale leaves 2 at a time, roll up into a cylinder, and thinly slice. (You should have about 4 cups of loosely packed kale.) Plunge the kale into the boiling water and cook for 1 minute.

Using a slotted spoon, transfer the kale to a colander and rinse under cold running water. Use your hands to squeeze out the excess moisture and set the kale aside.

Put the potatoes, sausage, and garlic into the same pot and bring to a boil. Reduce the heat to medium and simmer for about 15 minutes, or until the potatoes are tender. Remove the sausages to a platter and cover to keep warm. Drain the potatoes and garlic, reserving 1 cup of the cooking water. Mash the potatoes with the garlic using a ricer or food mill.

3 to 4 pounds chicken backs, necks, or wings

2 onions, quartered

2 carrots, thickly sliced

2 celery stalks, thickly sliced

2 bay leaves, crumbled

1 tablespoon chopped fresh thyme or 1 teaspoon dried thyme

1 tablespoon whole black peppercorns

1 teaspoon salt

Cold water

Return the potatoes to the pot, add the stock, and reheat. Stir in the kale and cook for 5 minutes longer. Season with salt and pepper and add the reserved potato water, a little at a time, until the desired consistency. Cut the sausage into ¼-inch-thick slices. Divide the sausage and bell pepper strips among large bowls, ladle in the soup, and serve. **SERVES 6**

CHICKEN STOCK

In a large pot, combine the chicken, onions, carrots, celery, bay leaves, thyme, peppercorns, and salt. Add enough cold water to cover by 1 inch. Bring to a boil, skimming off any froth that rises to the surface. Reduce the heat to medium and gently simmer, skimming often, for 3 to 4 hours.

Line a strainer with a double thickness of dampened cheesecloth, set over a large bowl, and pour the stock through. Discard the solids and skim off any fat from the surface. **MAKES 2 TO 3 QUARTS**

vietnamese lemongrass fish soup

Lemongrass, an essential ingredient in Vietnamese and Thai cooking, is available in Asian markets and specialty food stores. It imparts a refreshing citrus quality to the broth. You can also substitute grated lemon zest—the soup will be a little more pungent, but still quite good.

In a large heavy nonreactive pot, heat the oil over medium-high heat. Add the onion, celery, and lemongrass. Cook, stirring often, for 2 to 3 minutes, or until slightly softened. Add the cabbage and cook for 3 minutes, or until the cabbage is wilted. Stir in the stock and fish sauce, increase the heat to high, and bring to a boil. Season with salt and pepper and reduce the heat to medium-low. Add the fish and cook for 7 to 10 minutes, until the fish is opaque throughout.

Add the shrimp to the soup and cook for 1 minute longer. With a slotted spoon, transfer the fish and shrimp to large soup

2 tablespoons oil

1 small onion, finely chopped

1 celery stalk, peeled & thinly sliced

4 to 5 stalks lemongrass, trimmed & thinly sliced

1 cup thinly shredded cabbage, preferably bok choy

3 cups fish stock *(recipe follows)*

¼ cup bottled fish sauce, preferably nuoc mam,

Salt & freshly ground pepper

2 pounds lean white fish fillets, such as snapper, monkfish, or cod, skin removed & cut into large chunks

¾ pound small shrimp, peeled & deveined

bowls. Season the soup with salt and pepper if necessary. Add the snow peas and bring to a boil. Remove from the heat and stir in the lime juice and cilantro. Ladle the broth over the fish, garnish with the lime slices, and serve. **SERVES 4 TO 6**

15 snow peas, cut into fine julienne

2 tablespoons fresh lime juice

1 tablespoon chopped fresh cilantro

Lime slices, for garnish

FISH STOCK

In a large nonreactive pot, melt the butter over medium-high heat. Add the onion and cook, stirring often, for 3 to 5 minutes, until softened. Add the fish bones, water, wine, parsley, bay leaves, peppercorns, and salt. Bring to a boil, skimming off any froth that rises to the surface. Reduce the heat to medium and simmer for 20 minutes.

Line a strainer with a double thickness of dampened cheesecloth, set over a large bowl, and pour the stock through, discarding the solids. **MAKES ABOUT 1 QUART**

2 tablespoons butter

1 onion, finely chopped

2 pounds meaty bones from non-oily fish, such as cod or snapper, cut into large pieces

4 cups cold water

1 cup dry white wine

Fresh parsley sprigs

2 bay leaves, crumbled

10 whole black peppercorns

½ teaspoon salt

onion soup gratinée

Eighteen ½-inch-thick slices day-old French bread (from 1 medium-size baguette)

2 tablespoons unsalted butter, plus melted butter for drizzling

4 to 5 medium-size Vidalia onions (about 2 pounds), halved & thinly sliced

6 cups beef stock (p. 79) or broth

Salt & freshly ground pepper

¾ cup grated Gruyère or other Swiss cheese (about 6 ounces)

Hearty homemade beef stock is best for this comfort soup. The cheese topping makes it fairly rich, but served alongside a crisp green salad, it becomes a perfect late-night supper.

Preheat the oven to 350°F. Arrange the bread in a single layer on a baking sheet. Bake, turning once or twice, for 15 to 20 minutes, until the bread is dry and lightly browned. Set aside.

In a large heavy pot, melt the butter over medium-high heat. Add the onions and reduce the heat to medium-low. Cook, stirring often, for 15 to 20 minutes, until the onions are very soft and golden brown. Pour in the stock and season to taste with salt and pepper. Bring to a simmer and cook for 10 to 15 minutes, until the flavors have blended.

Preheat the broiler. Arrange the slices of bread in individual ovenproof bowls. Ladle in the hot soup, sprinkle evenly with the cheese, and drizzle with butter. Broil, 4 to 6 inches from the source of heat, for 2 to 3 minutes, until the cheese is browned.

SERVES 6

swedish yellow split pea soup

This Scandinavian favorite is traditionally served with dark rye bread. Here the bread is made into croutons, which provide an interesting texture counterpoint to the pureed soup.

In a large pot, melt the butter over medium-high heat. Add the carrot, onion, celery, and potato. Cook for 5 minutes, or until the onion is softened. Stir in the split peas and stock and increase the heat to high. Bring to a boil, then reduce the heat to medium-low. Simmer, partially covered, stirring, for 1 hour, or until the split peas are soft and falling apart.

In a food processor or blender, puree the soup in batches. Return the soup to the pot, stir in the mustard, and season with the cumin, salt, and pepper. Reheat, then ladle into small bowls and top with the croutons. **SERVES 4**

2 tablespoons unsalted butter

1 large carrot, chopped

1 large onion, chopped

1 celery stalk, chopped

1 medium-size all-purpose potato (6 to 8 ounces), peeled & cut into 1-inch cubes

1 cup yellow split peas, picked over & rinsed

4 cups vegetable stock (p. 77) or broth

1 tablespoon Dijon mustard, or more to taste

1 teaspoon ground cumin

Salt & freshly ground pepper

Dark rye bread croutons, for serving (p. 52)

2 tablespoons olive oil

1 large onion, chopped

1 celery stalk, chopped

2 teaspoons mild curry powder, or more to taste

½ pound lentils, (about 1¼ cups), picked over & rinsed

4 cups vegetable stock *(recipe follows)*, **chicken stock (p. 70) or broth, plus additional if needed**

Salt & freshly ground pepper

Caramelized onions (p. 33), for garnish (optional)

Curry powder, a blend of up to twenty herbs and spices, is an ideal match for lentils. Serve small portions of this hearty soup with grilled poppadums, followed by oven-roasted fish and steamed seasonal vegetables.

In a large heavy pot, heat the oil over medium-high heat. Add the onion and celery and cook, stirring, for 3 to 5 minutes, until the onion is softened. Stir in the curry powder and cook, stirring, for 1 minute longer.

Add the lentils and stock to the pot. Bring to a boil over high heat. Reduce the heat to medium and simmer for 35 to 45 minutes, until the lentils are tender, adding additional stock or water if needed to keep the lentils covered by about 1 inch of water. Season with salt and pepper.

In a food processor or blender, puree half the soup. Return the puree to the soup in the pot and reheat, thinning the soup with additional stock or water, if desired. Season to taste with salt and pepper. Ladle into small bowls and top with the caramelized onions, if using. **SERVES 4**

VEGETABLE STOCK

In a large pot, combine the onions, carrots, celery, leeks, turnip, bay leaf, thyme, peppercorns, and salt. Pour in enough cold water to cover by about 1 inch. Bring the water to a boil over medium-high heat. Reduce the heat and simmer, uncovered, for about 2 hours, adding the potatoes during the last hour of cooking time.

Line a strainer with a double thickness of dampened cheesecloth, set over a large bowl, and pour the stock through, discarding the solids.

MAKES 1 TO 1½ QUARTS

2 onions, quartered

2 carrots, thickly sliced

2 celery stalks, thickly sliced

2 leeks (white part only), halved lengthwise & washed well

1 turnip, quartered

1 bay leaf, crumbled

Several fresh thyme sprigs

10 whole black peppercorns

1 teaspoon salt

Cold water

1 pound all-purpose potatoes, peeled & cut into ¾-inch chunks

hungarian goulash soup

2 tablespoons butter

2 tablespoons oil

1½ pounds boneless beef round, chuck, or sirloin, cut into 1-inch cubes

Salt & freshly ground pepper

1 large onion, chopped

1 each red & green bell pepper, halved, cored, seeded & chopped

1 medium-size tomato, seeded & chopped

1 tablespoon paprika, preferably Hungarian

2 tablespoons all-purpose flour

4 cups beef stock *(recipe follows)* **or broth**

Sour cream, for garnish

Variations of this robust soup have been prepared in Hungary since the ninth century. For the most authentic results, use imported sweet paprika.

In a large nonreactive pot, melt the butter with the oil over medium-high heat. Season the beef with salt and pepper, add to the pot and cook, turning, for 10 minutes, or until the beef is no longer pink. Drain on a paper towel–lined plate.

Pour off all but 2 tablespoons of the fat from the pot. Add the onion and bell peppers and cook, stirring, for 5 minutes, or until softened. Return the beef to the pot. Stir in the tomato and paprika and sprinkle with the flour. Cook, stirring, for 7 to 10 minutes, until the juices are thickened and glossy.

Stir in the stock, increase the heat to high, and bring to a boil. Season with salt and pepper. Reduce the heat to medium-low and cook, partially covered, for 1 to 1½ hours, until the beef is very tender, skimming off any fat from the surface.

Ladle the soup into large shallow bowls and garnish each serving with a dollop of sour cream. **SERVES 4 TO 6**

BEEF STOCK

Preheat the oven to 450°F. Put the bones in a roasting pan and roast, turning the bones occasionally, for 30 to 40 minutes, or until well browned. Add the onions, carrots, and celery and roast for about 15 minutes, or until browned.

Transfer the bones and vegetables to a large stockpot. Pour off and discard the fat from the roasting pan. Place the pan on top of the stove and pour in 2 cups water. Deglaze the pan by bringing the water to a boil and scraping to loosen any browned bits in the pan. Pour the liquid into the pot. Add the remaining ingredients and enough cold water to cover by 1 inch. Bring to a boil, skimming off any froth. Reduce the heat and barely simmer, skimming often, for 4 to 5 hours, until the stock is rich tasting.

Line a strainer with a double thickness of dampened cheesecloth, set over a large bowl, and pour the stock through, skimming of any fat. Discard the solids.

MAKES ABOUT 3 QUARTS

3 pounds meaty beef bones

2 onions, quartered

2 carrots, thickly sliced

2 celery stalks, thickly sliced

About 16 cups cold water

2 medium-size tomatoes, seeded & chopped

1 bay leaf, crumbled

Several fresh parsley stems

1 fresh thyme sprig

1 garlic clove, crushed

10 whole black peppercorns

1 teaspoon salt

index